VOICES & VENUES In VERSE!

Sunflowers, GOD's Gift & Prize

Partnered with:
Bees, Trees & Butterflies
& White Sails, in God's Blue Sky!

By -
Kenneth J. Hesterberg

Copyright © 2024 by Kenneth J. Hesterberg

All rights reserved.

ISBN 978-1-62806-429-2

Library of Congress Control Number 2024919600

Published by Salt Water Media
29 Broad Street, Suite 104
Berlin, MD 21811
www.saltwatermedia.com

Cover photos courtesy of:
P/Lt Lawrence G. Davies, Cambridge Sail and Power Squadron

Primary Editor: Janet Jones

(In sadness say, both have passed in the autumn of 2023.)

Gifts, From GOD

Take, the beautiful Sun Flower, in fields' bright array,
Whose seeds, when harvested, provide, a tasty treat,
by humans, In numbers of delightful ways.
Then include; Bees, Trees & Butterflies__
For, the Honey-Bee, the beautiful tree,
And, the seeming, delicate, butterfly;
what strength, they exhibit every day__
Pollenating what God, tasks of them to do.

And note, rivers, where boats do ply,
With, sails unfurled, radiant white, in;
God's blue sky, bring warm feelings inside.
Keep in mind; what GOD would have__
Humankind do; if they but heeded,
the word; Brotherhood; is right.
Noting, internal organs, by blood match,
were interchangeable__ so, let not___
the "tint" of skin dictate; with whom,
each will abide, for all humans are:
From. the "same: "Tree of Life." Are we, not?

A Brother and Sister, to every other__
And, a friend to all where, ere they abide,
Could then WAR, be, no longer__
And humankind not ride___ Satan's coat-tail;
To certain death and destruction?
Tis a shame, humans can't, or could they, if they tried?
So many things, in life's parade;
Add, beauty and worth, to the hours,
granted to we humans each day.
Worth the thinking of what life could/should be.

If, but humankind truly accepts each other as family.

A Word More

How great the Gifts that God provides,
They make, life worth living,
In, good times. and times of trial.
Find them, throughout. this Orb we ride.

More to remember and digest__
What about the sail, like a flag unfurled__

Or, the artist, whose colors bring life alive,
And, the music, that is played and sung?

It takes, more than a village to raise, a child__
This, is, the whole Worlds' job.

A thought to preserve: no one alive today,
Can claim innocence, in humankinds' sins__
Of, Global Warming, Climate Change and plastic pollution of the world's Oceans. Tis we, everyone, must roll up our sleeves to save; life on this Orb.

God's gifts are there, but we must show__ we care.

Dedication

To one who has done a lifetime of good,
with few ripples in the tides of Life,
Note is taken, and gratitude given:
To: a good friend, and avid Reader;

To:

Richard "Dick" Elzey

A man for all seasons!

Our Orb in the Universe

I lean, on you__
Because I can, in this moment in time.
The ink and paper are mine.
Until the moment is gone.
And then, you are again, on your own.
Like a "King or Queen" of your own domain__
For scant moments in time.
And then__ you again,
Are "**threads**," in the "**Tapestry**" of life.

But think not, for that is no small thing__
Like the Bee, and the Butterfly,
Who pollinate, most every plant, on Earth__
Or the Tree, and its brothers and sisters__
Most, everywhere to be seen.
"**Venting**," life giving gasses into the air.
Playing a role, "without" which;
Humankind, most likely__ would disappear.
Each has an important part, to play.
And, many times, adjusting to needed change.

Remember, as far as we know,
None of, humankind, now living, are a: "GOD."
(Although, many like to think they are.)
We, in reality, are like everyone, else__
If you will: "**Worker Bees.**"
"**Caretakers**" of this Planet__
Forget that not. **For if you do,**
Future, generations, will put their curse on you.
For this, is their inheritance__
That you are charged; in & for its care!

Table of Contents

Prologue	13
Family Matters	14
In a Nutshell	16
Our World of When	17
Self-Examination	18
Receive & Respond	19
The Battered Book	20
The Epilog Scribed	28
Meaning of Words	29
Moments with the Master	30
Moments from Yesterday	31
Weather all the Time	32
Retrospective	33
Luck of the Draw	34
The Measure of a Book	36
That Girl	37
The Keeper	38
Fact of Life	39
A Soldier's Day	40
Observation	41
Waking of the Mind	41
A Sailor's Dilemma	42
Moments Not Wasted	43
A Boater's Reverie	44
Vista Scene	45

Tinkering with Time	46
Tinkering with Time Chapter 2	47
Tinkering With Time Chapter 3	50
Nothing is Forever	52
The Essence of Time	53
Each, a Story to Tell	54
The Feeling Within	55
Cover Under the Stars	56
Better to be Good	57
Future Review	58
Realization	59
Chesapeake Icon	60
Following the Theme	62
A Reminder in Time	63
A Thought Given	64
Time and Travel	65
A Dog's Tale, or Tail!	66
Family Christmas	68
The Wild West	69
A Verse-ist Sharing's	70
Observation	71
Idea Reception	72
Eye, on the "Race(s)"	73
Carried Pieces	74
Stormy Night	76
Life Facts	78
Counting Time	79

A Woman in My Life	80
Thought Messenger	81
Sustenance	82
Winter, on the Bay	83
To Understand	84
Selection	85
Shakespeare Maybe	86
Who Says	87
Winter Walking	88
If, It Could Be	90
Discipline, Makes It So	91
Smile Remembered	92
History if not Accepted	94
Words, Somewhat Like	95
That Book	96
Those Days	98
When the Time Comes	99
Moments of Growth	100
Spyglass on Life	102
The Gift of Gifts	103
The Man I Am	104

Other Books by KJH in the series: VOICES & VENUES IN VERSE!

The World of Water: Fair winds and foul, beacons, lighthouses, on ocean, rivers and bays, or in the deep!

Yesterdays, Other Days and Holidays: Holiday's of humankind, Tributes, Recognitions & Remembrances!

Inspiration: Thoughts the additive, for the engine of humankind!

Inspiration Two & Too: Self-motivation through life!

Moments in Time and Scope: Memories, ideas, capacity for achievement, vastness for self!

Of People and Spaces: Space like most things in life, only a restriction of the human self!

Choices, Chances & Life: Choices- to make! Chances__ one takes! Life__ a gift of worth!

VISTAS: Visions of the beholder, seen, felt & sensed, memory markers!

Tapestry of Life Spun: Woven through ones life, how good when done, depends on the path chosen!

Earth Tones: Majestic in color & sound, there, where ere you go__ your gift!

Earth Rhythms: Earth's rhythms playing on this planet's scene, there to grab and hold!

Rebound: A skill to perfect, to better your life!

Baker's Dozen: When a Dozen, become 13, with short stories in Verse, to touch, your heart, soul and mind!

XIV: A tribute to days when numbers, were letters, and no zeros could be found!

The Gathering: Of, like groups human and non-human, together find a kindred ship!

Perambulation: If you think you are not in life's parade, how foolish you are!

Perception: A gift at birth, helping to make each day the best it can be!

Diversity: Life's colors, sounds, feelings and times!

Intuition: Perhaps a touch of magic, or ESP, or remnants found in one's DNA!

Mélange: This, that and the other", to capture your invested moments!

Turns: Actions that influence the direction of life!

A Moment in Time: Are gems to hold and serve for a lifetime.

Sunflowers, God's Gift & Prize

<u>The following, written and awaiting publication!</u>
"The Time Before" The springboard, for all of life's days to come.
Tomorrow's Run completion to gain in the next 24

Cover photos of all Books, in the series; except, "Perambulation & Sun Flowers" are waters of, & near, the Chesapeake Bay__
"My, muse. My Books, not novels, but "Short & Longer, Stories in verse." written, to be read, throughout life!

Prologue

From Family Christmas letters,
With, one column_ verses about "Santa"
Never did I expect a book of Verse to write_
Then at my "Brides" passing,
The thinking, was: a book; "One and done."
See the page above,
And, note how much ink, I have spread.

The first sixteen, were published in order,
And, then with five more, ready for publishing,
Timeliness of subject came to the fore,
Of course, my age, its role did play.

Then, 2023, a year many changes_
Touched my life, two that autumn,
were the passing of Janet Jones,
the Editor of many of my books,
And, Larry Davies, Photographer,
of many of my book covers.,
Dear friends., missed and remembered.

This is the 23 Book of mind, published,
And in the Library of Congress;
and never at one time, thought that to be.
A bit of ego, I wonder what_
my wife, mother and dad would say?
The effort has been pure enjoyment,
much work, time and hopefully,
good reading for many, and dollars,
for the not-for-profits, I try to help support.
And, if GOD is willing, a book or two more!

Family Matters
(A tale, all true in its way.)

From my window, I did see,
The darkness of night, turn gray__
And from the East,
A bit of sunlight' did play.

I watched as "Old Sol"
Climbed higher in the sky__
Till it was full round,
And, a ball of red, peering down.

I could not help, but smile a bit,
For I was alive, for another daily trip__
How much more time,
Could I successfully grab?

And, did I want to be, like, my dad__
Who, a full century did see?

That "old bugger" was__
Still chasing women at 85.

That I know, cause, I had to go,
To court, as that young woman,
Asked support, for my new half-brother.

My old man, said, with a glint in his eye,
"How many more can I make__
In the time, I am still alive?
And, we thought the judge, would surely choke.

Well, Dad was more careful,
After that__ and got around pretty good,
For sixteen more years, till 101,
He just had himself a lot of fun.
Funny how life goes around,
I married that gal, so dad stayed out of jail,
And, she has been a fine wife to me,
Even though, I'm 20 years older than she.

And, me now__ on my way__
To that century mark,
Which I won't make, cancers got me marked.
And my grandkids,
Think, my life is a lark!
They should have known__ their great grandpa.

And, to them all, I've said goodbye,
Over a period of time__
And, I spent many "ticks of the clock,"
With, that half-brother, adopted son, of mine__
Close we've been all his living time.
- - - - -
I found most of these words,
In notes my step dad had jotted down.
And, now around his hospital bed,
We all sort of packed in.
My, mom, his wife, a tear in her eye,
Me her son, and his half-brother/son__
Said, with a smile: " that dad of mine__
Was, a "hell of a guy"
And, we all laughed!

And my mom his wife leaned over,
And kissed his brow,

And said, you my love:
A better man, you are__ all around!
She now at 66__
Married again__ no and never,
Me__ married with a family,
And, a passel of kids;
And a good life has had, and a fine step-dad,
And him, my half-brother, too.

"Some families are truly a "hoot"
It really doesn't matter where you start,
It's how you play the game of life__
And, the good you do, each day you age__
And, he, my dad, and half- brother,
Both in time, and A better man, you cannot find.

Ah, families, what's in the closet, there is to find?

In a Nutshell

Living life, is a never- ending- fight,
Some times with the gloves on,
But most times,
There are no gloves in sight.

So, biting and gouging,
Many deem to be right.
Too bad all don't see,
The better "plan" GOD, has put in sight.

You remember GOD, don't you?
He's is the one with the son; who walks on water:

Our World of When

Instead of waiting to call,
I am dropping a line to you.
And, bringing back,
A memory, of the time__
Of notes and letters,
Once crafted and mailed,
With a three-cent stamp.
To say Thank You,
For an effort or gift sent.
Remember, when a three-cent stamp,
Or a penny post card,
Told another, you truly cared?

Of course, not, most of you will say__
That was before your time.
And I would understand.
For, they, were also days,
Of nickers and pinafores;
And, Street Cars on tracks,
And, 13 buns, making a dozen.
GI's, back from WW2.
And, people saying: "yes Sir or no Ma'am,"
Or, please and thank you.

I am not saying, a better world, but different.
One not to be seen again, one that____
You should, know and be, reminded of.
And, those that were there__
Yes, those few__ still alive from that era__
A pretty good bunch, if I say so myself;
And those, they some, of your ancestors too.

Self-Examination

My weaknesses, like many, I think,
Are things I truly deplore __
Some because I have little interest in__
Others because I lack the smarts to employ.
And still others, I question__
Why, anyone, would invest, their time__
On people with bad breath,
Expelling so much "Hot Air, "just wasting time.

Take the plethora of politicians,
Spewing speeches every day__
They open their mouths__
And, their petition to us,
Is to give them our money__
So once elected, little work will they face.
(Well maybe__ not all of them?)

Wait, these are not, weaknesses,
They are just irritations,
Or agitations that bug me a lot!
These things (plus others) in which,
I have no interest; come from people__
For whom, I care little about.

So here is what I suggest,
Bother me not with your banter,
If you have, an idea you think is a dandy__
Write it up in detail and mail it to me;
But kindly, leave off the stamp.

And then, wait for a reply,

Then, the happiest, of the two of us__
Will be__ "me, of should that be I?"
So, perhaps my weaknesses, are fewer in number?
Maybe I am a pretty smart guy?
Too smart to be hoodwinked by you,
So, if I like, the, person, you are__
Maybe a job as a "honey-dipper," you'll try,
And do something worthwhile__
Like making "crap" disappear; as, you smile.

"I think__ I'm becoming, a Curmudgeon__ aren't, I?

Receive & Respond

Do, and did you realize__
How much we owe to others,
And, many of those__ we do not know?
Others, who have invested,
Maybe unknowingly__
In our lives, throughout our gift of life,
I guess we could say__ as part, of their legacy.

This is the way of life__ borrow from the older__
And then a legacy leave for the new,
And, if all goes well, each new generation;
Will get and then provide__
To make this world, a better place.
For many, in time, yet unknown.

"**Point Clarified:**" *Take all that is offered.*
Use what you take, and leave more than you took__
To assure, a better world__ than you found.
This, a life legacy, to repay, for breath received.
Throughout the time of living

The Battered Book
(A tale to ponder)

I couldn't sleep,
So, with the sun peeping over the horizon,
I went downstairs, through the clutter__
Of, mounds of cardboard boxes,
Holding, the good, useable, saleable,
and trash-able, history, of thirty years__
Of residency in this our home.

Moving day was, 24 hours closer now.
I, began quietly to haul plastic bags,
Boxes, trash barrels, and loose stuff,
To the curb for today's, pick-up.
Other boxes carefully labeled and sorted,
With the kid's (no longer kids)
Addresses attached, ready for shipment__
Far and wide, across this country.

Never thought we, this distance of separation,
Of our close-knit clan would ever be__
From, this "land" of our ancestors.
And, in this day and time,
With the younger version, of she and I,
Four corners of the country spread,
And, the fifth in Europe to be found.

We, the wife & I, still in love__ separating also.
It was only right, both having dreams to try.
What with kids, and professions, and life,
And the challenges of a large family,
It took thirty years, and early retirement;

And mutual agreement, that we should __
While time was still on our side__
I let the black cloud, pass,
And got myself back on track,
There was another big pile in the next room,
My "bride" said to review and dispatch.

There was catch in her voice as she said that.
So, I guessed, it was pieces of our life together,
That could still hold sway,
Before it too, was to be cast away!
- - - -
And there it sat!
With finger smudges, and juice stains,
And, sweat spots from warmer days,
And, pages scotch taped back in,
And, years where untouched it stayed,
On the shelf, dusted with feathers,
Along, with others__
And then the rug, vacuumed,
And then left in solitude, again.

Its cover torn and frayed,
And, seeming ready for a book graveyard,
Is what I first saw this day. as memories returned,
When that book, came my, families' way__
Those, many years, ago.

I remembered, it as a gift,
Christmas paper from a Grand Mother, old,
Who passed away, some years ago.
And a note in her handwriting___
That stuck in my mind, these many years past.

"You always loved this one, "Little Man"

My, nick name, in the time ago__
"And with my time near,
I thought you might like to share,
With the off springs, that__ come your way."
"And I send it now
Before the "vultures" come to prey,
On what's left of these old bones,
When, my time is finally gone."
And, I could see her laughing,
And that smile, and those eyes__
Deep pool blue.
She was a feisty old "bird."
And so much love, she shared,
In those days, once in time, just us two.

It was__ a "Children's Book" in its way.
Written in a style now passé'
Written by a relative,
An educated man, who lived his life,
In the wilderness of a new country,
Not yet, to find its way__
But, searching, differences in the world to do.

But oh, what a book it was __It was, an old book,
even then, and had been read, many times,
In a century, long closed, before my birth.

The art in sketches. still alive this day.
And, had been read to me,
Before reading caught my attention,
And became, one of my avid pursuits__

Well into my teen years,
In visits to that grandmother, I loved so.
Let me tell you what I see,

In this now dirty and tattered tome__
It is, a history, of a large family tree;
Of boys and girls now grown and gone.
Who in an adventure, spun, saw themselves;
in lines, and page, on mountain trails,
And raging rivers__ a book, hard, to ever put down.
which, taught more than their ABCs__
About life, and living in a world,
Lost, to the likes of us.

That ancestor, had an infinity,
To animals of all types,
From small to truly large,
And they with names given,
Played a large role throughout the pages,
From first, to the end,
And, felt, so, much captured truth, was inked.

And for many, even as teen years came their way
It at times was picked-up again,
And thumbed through, and remembered__
As a "friend" who started many a kid,
On the right path__ to stay.
Of knowledge well taught,
To carry one on life's way__
And, characters that history made.

How old the book,
Lost on pages somewhere in time
No one can find, when the year written,
Was inked in place.
But a marvel even today.
It was in a pile now,
A large pile, to be "trashed-canned,"
And, sent on its way,

And, I knew this would never do,
As did my wife, tis why,
She left the final decision, me to decide.

I looked up, as she came in the door.
"I should have known; you would find it__"
And, I said: "not a thing you should have done."
A bit of anger flashed in my words.
And, "yes she said, I came down __
To rescue it, again!"

In somewhat of a snit,
The book, I gathered in,
And, wended my way, through boxes
Already packed for the move,
Of shipping, and trashing, and donating__
And decisions never thought to make,
From this our once family home,
Where pets and kids, were seen and heard.

All that could wait; for in my mind now,
Was a job to be done.
And, to my workshop,
In, the basement, down below__
To be done__ it would be__
Before this house to leave.

She following me down,
No words needed to be said,
And I turned, and held her close,
And tears we both shed,
Leaving this "home' was a very hard blow.
As was this book, from long ago,
In its way, was the glue to the life we both knew.

A "Key Stone" cut those many years ago!
Together then, as so many times before,
She to her studio, art to make,
Me to the shop, materials to find,
And tools align, and space to work.

And, funny how we knew,
Art and wood, a different, cover to view!
And the laser cut, making beauty new.
We got to work, to make better a gem of old.
Soon, the book, to be passed old but new.
To family, as it had been passed__
In decades, before.
But now, family to be, spread__ hither and yon__
And, that not even considering
The ones beyond our former household.

Some pages we remade
Following the style therein,
And minor marked, the old and new.
And, the cover would open,
And the pages well laid,
Easy to read, the story old and true.
Hard not to get drawn, in,
How well we remembered__ how well.

And, the spots, and stains,
And even ink marks,
Seemed right in places found.

And, she looked at me, and I at, her;
How fitting it seemed, this job together__
Was, so perfect an ending__
Before a new beginning__ begun.
Someday; one day, together again__

If the plans, made were, done.

The kids began arriving,
All of us in a hotel, tonight, would stay;
But now, to wander, the house, our once home.

Stuff, to "four corners and Europe,
Shipped and gone,
Then an afternoon, of visiting around.
Many families and friends,
Likely to see very seldom again.

All together_ then for the evening meal_
Then she and I showed them the book.
And the two with grand kids,
Started the reading off, and then the others_
And its wonder did work,
Attention was rife, as always had been.
And, the little ones paid attention,
Till the "Sandman," took them down.
The oldest son, the book got to share around.

We then explained further our plan!
My Bride to NY to show and paint her art,
Living with in an apartment, with studio there,
And me, in the boat with sail,
Europe to be my first port of call.
But room in each, for the other,
When together again, heard the call.

The kids were first, put off,
Until, somewhat could see,
We stayed together, and would always be!

On the roof top, in the dark of night,

With less and less ambient light,
Stars somewhat filled the sky,
And a comet streaked across, passing us by.
And, we watched, holding tight,
And felt then all was right.

And, "A Battered Book, In our son's hands__
Ready, for another century of family to find.
Who knows, what each tomorrow will bring;
Memories strong and family ties__
Hopefully, a true thing!

Each, in the family, to write a log,
And, by yearend, copies sent to everyone__
Perhaps from these, a new book__
With tales as good as the ancestor had done,
In this, now different world__
Ours for a time.

But we like they___ had dreams to fulfill.
And, life too short, an effort not to put in.

And, gather we, for breakfast, one more time.
It was then, now for all to go their way!
Hugs, tears, and the promise __
of a new tomorrow.
And all a fair time, with__

"The Battered Book"
A true family Treasure again survived.

If God is but willing, and life allows.
may, someday, we all are together__
in the same place and time again__
Amen__ Little Man!

The Epilog Scribed

So, a new cover, carefully contrived__
A very new ambience soon to be read;
By many alive!
But, even with a cover new,
Like a beautiful face on the screen,
The true beauty of a person or thing,
Is that which is captured, inside;
It was the time and the gist, of the story__
Of family members, to leave land well known.
And cross a sea to make history,
In a new place, to become, known.
And again, centuries on, a repeat, in its way__

Can do each, and every day.
And not like, a once handsome exterior__
Aging, and time; call for the "Piper to be paid.
Inside beauty is truly the look, to gage.

And, The Battered Book
Worth every moment, it takes to read.
The patina,
The, look of a gift,
Of, generations gone,
With love added in__
To enhance the story,
That, the good ancestor,
First had seen and lived,
In the untouched beauty
Of the land of red men,
Cougar, perhaps even,
The last mastodon.

Natural made ink,
Firelight applied__
I hope, each generation of my kin__
Eke out the time, to get to know__
The history of those ancestors,
And find, they are well worth,
the time to know.

Meaning of Words

There was a time,
When in jest, called a friend__
An "A-hole!" he looked at me with a big grin,
And, said thanks; for a great compliment.
And kept grinning, but said not a word more.
While I kept waiting, for a bitter retort.
Then he started to walk away__
"Whoa" said I__ he grinned even wider.

"In your naiveté, said he,
You realized not, the "A" Hole, without__
We alive would, not be.
And then he did walk away,

And, put me to thinking, how right he was.
That, the one who calls another,
A name like that, in discourse given__
Is most likely unwittingly,
The bigger "Ass" of the two!
As he/she gave, a complement,
that never meant to do.

Clarity of content; is a prime factor, *of first, to review.*

Moments with the Master

One can learn much, if willing to sit,
In the shade of a tree, and enjoy the cool,
Of a warm summer day,
And watch a colony of ants,
By the hundreds, do, what ants do.
The brilliance of movement, wasting little,
of energy, that gets them the needed,

Till that particular job is done.
And then those in the colony,
can be seen no more, but others,
have come to the fore,
and then the song of a Lark or a Cardinal,
Of both in a time, bring a smile,
And for minutes in time sing different notes,
That blend, as other birds do join.
And the longer you pause,
in that, afternoon time,
So much can you see, hear and find__
And even will wonder, why more moments,
Such as these you seldom allow in life. _
For, there is no end to learning,
If an, open mind is given time__

To garner knowledge worth to share,
With & for, the benefit of "all "earthy folk.
As the goal to learn more, comes to bear__
How foolish human kind, to take not the time,
To sit at God's feet, and take in__
The lessons provided, along with the new "**A-I**.'
For, if not. a Correction, of Direction__
Can we on this ORB, survive?

Moments from Yesterday

I remember only too well,
The party line phones,
I was first taught to use,
In the era ending__
The Great Depression!
This, to impress you of my memory,
Of that time back then,

It was a black phone, no other color seen.
And, one step away from__ an earpiece,
on a wire of its own!
And when picked up to call,
You had to listen quickly,
To assure your party,
Wasn't on the line, saying: "Off".

When finally, the line was clear,
The Telephone Operator,
Said Loudly: In your ear:
"Number Please"__
And, then it was your turn,
To say: "Get off of the Line!

Then came World War 2,
And when done, new phones__
With, dial tones came!
And, our number Gilmore 2358 J__
Now, Cell phones, in pockets,
Or purses, cluttering up,
A life, we once knew.
Some changes, aren't bad, note I said some

Weather all the Time

Cold, they said, the day would be__
Perhaps sun and a breeze to rattle leaves,
With, cold and wind, I am okay__
But, with a full gale, a price to pay.
True, it was late fall, soon, winter to arrive.
But for me, too soon for the snow,

Soon it was to be__ Turkey Day!
Not more than a week away;
And with my taste buds well primed,
For, fresh ham, my choice, turkey go away.

But, others like the traditional bird__
Golden brown, to arrive at table time.
With dressing flavorful lodged inside__
And, all the trimmings, to be supplied.

But you can have my turkey share,
If the aroma of "fresh ham, "is filling the air.
Makes me, wonder why, the turkey__
Not, the wiser pig__ ever got anywhere.
Well, if for Thanksgiving, I get no ham__
I will ask Santa, for a gift, that I demand,
That on the table Christmas Day,
Fresh ham and sauerkraut__ will be displayed.

I have been a good boy__
Few bad marks on my record engraved,
So why not those, "turkey gobblers,"
Join me, for an even taster meal arrayed?
With, mashed potatoes, gravy and pie; Oh My!

Retrospective

Tis funny, as you entertain,
The enlightenment, that comes into life___
Unfolding before your eyes,
The exploding of knowledge,
Seeming, new to you__
That perhaps you should have known,

But, never did it dawn, on you,
Until, this moment, and in this time.
But, now, with suddenness,
Sparks of color,
In kaleidoscopic bits flashing
Come with the speed of light.
Opening your mind,

And, with acceptance__
Your brain grasps full meaning
Of ideas once foreign in your sight.

This proves once again,
The facile abilities of the human brain__
In its effort to cope,
With complex situations.

But, knowing not what tomorrow brings,
If, there is to be, a tomorrow?
Humankinds' misuse, of Planet Earth__
Must be reversed__ as a prerequisite.
"This, but Common Sense, applied!"

To save, the "Earth;" for those not yet alive!

Luck of the Draw

I was now in New England,
And the frost had been,
On the pumpkins, for some while.
In fact, the snow "high above the curbs,
When finally, I did arrive.

The office building, I was to call home__
Was, over 100 years young, and it showed.
And, repairs needed__ oblivious to every eye.
Like the 8" diameter ice cycle,
From, the soffit, above the second floor,
To the ground in the parking lot__
Shimmering in the streetlights.

But this, was just one, of many surprises,
In time to be found;
However; this and that, came with the job,
And, a job, I liked.
And stayed, from the late 70's__
Until the mid 80s,
Then, more of New England found.

Now in the years, I was there,
So, many challenges and adventures__
Filled the hours, days and those years__
Too many to detail, for not enough__
Paper and time, can I spare!
But I want to share a bit about,
A man, who became a friend, that first year.

A meeting, just one of many__

That makes life, worth the time to stay alive.
John Barton his name, much older than I__
And, would assume, at my age now, John__
Is growing flowers, in God's domicile.

For, growing flowers,
Was, john's fancy, and his profession.
That first time, I entered his greenhouses,
It took my breath away, for acres of flowers there__
Made one believe even more so,
In God's loving ways!

I had missed Christmas,
For in January I did arrive,
But with Easter the color so alive,
And later, Azaleas __ to catch the eye,
And, then fall flowers.

Before long, it was Christmas in the air.
Yes, November came__
And, his greenhouses were alive__
With Poinsettias__
Colored those Green Houses in beauty and pride!
Oh, each time I entered,
My breath was held at bay,
For the red, brightened, those chilly days.

My wife was the flower person of our family,
Trees I knew somewhat, and, the grass I did cut,
But, when I met John,
In his cave of an office,
A feeling inside__ made me blush!

John was like his flowers,
A man with a "bloom' you could trust.

He made life a little better,
For each soul he touched.
Our friendship lasted for years,
And, I missed him, when we moved far away__
And, unfortunately, I saw him no more.
But, think of him, when I see a flower,
And, his memory__ stays fresh,
On my life's way.
Perhaps, if I am lucky,
He and I will again chat__ on some future day.

There is much more I could tell you,
Like his love and service in Scouting,
But hopefully a picture you get!

A truly good man! A true gentleman__
Whose generosity spread near and far.
A New Englander, in culture,
Having him as a friend, a true bonus,
Of my professional life.

The Measure of a Book

A thought to keep, as pages you turn,
For, tis soon time to rest your eyes.

You need no Critic, to tell you_
The value of a book.
For, you will know it's worth__

When the ending is nigh;
It is never to apply,
Too good, was every word and line.

That Girl

I think often, of my long-gone bride.
Missing her and her always wise council,
Sends me into a pall, of regret.
Her passing before me,
Was never the plan!

And, while our marriage,
Spanned more than, five decades,
The years flew by too fast.
And here I, have spent___
Another, decade, asking why;
It was she to go___ and not I?

I think of this often,
And these lines flood my mind:
"Life, is a measured moment in time."
For humankind, and all species,
Never, if ever announced,
Till the end is deemed doable or done.
And yet that date in stone, is etched.

I wonder if a vote be taken,
How badly, nay to a change,
Humankind, would respond?
I guess, it is still best___
To, accept the time granted;
with an unknown date;
than one, that is noted to anticipate.

Always, thinking of you, "My Girl."
Always…

The Keeper

The TV on__ brought to mind,
A path once taken,
Near seven decades ago.
When, perhaps, a wrong choice made__
In the year, 1954.

My, bride to be, and I,
Opened a joint savings account,
This against the odds,
Was to prove quite right.
With a plan to put away,
Enough money together, to purchase,
Our furniture, without debt__
We did and done.

Each on a finger__
We wore the others' high school ring,
And, I, not one with thought to, jewelry,
We agreed, this our engagement__
Did and had made.
Now, these, many years later__

I more than wonder, If, perhaps, was wrong?
She never said so__
And later down the line,
Some fine, jewelry, she enjoyed.

Funny, I think of this now,
For, when comes the ides of August,
She will be gone eleven years__
And if still alive, on the Ides of October,

Our, 69th, wedding anniversary would be.
Far too short a time, I feel those days.
Perhaps, this is just a case,
Of, too late__ smart, too soon old.
We each had a gold Wedding ring,
Hers she wore for those near 58 years,
And me, for 64 till arthritis said no more!
Into a spot, that gold will shine,
Just on my finger, now it is gone.

A keeper, she was!
And, I pray, not, no never__
Lose her in my memory.
A diamond on her finger deserved,
And, though she a diamond got later,
I pray she forgave me,
For what I didn't do, when should have.

"What, is the measure of time_
If not the good days,
Out numbering, all others.
Of knowing how lucky you were,
When the "dice of life" were rolled."

Fact of Life

Get old, or get dead__
There, is really no other choice;
This is Natures' way.
You are, aware; Nature is Boss?
Too bad humankind, sees this not__
How much time, and frustration;
Would be saved throughout life__
If to Nature humans__ would just heed.

A Soldier's Day

It wasn't the time, but it was the day.
It wasn't the place, but not far away__
And, it was supposed__ to be others,
For it was their turn,
But there I was__ facing the enemy.

And all in my gun sight__
And in a few seconds gone__
I took their lives away.
Because it was them__ or me.

A soldier, no choice has__
In War, when, politicians__
Think the game, is theirs' __ to play.
But I am long enough here__
And War have faced,
With little chance to sleep
And Morpheus', soon chased that away.

Maybe if lucky,
Alive, I will be for another day__
And another, after that;
Oh, just home__ I want to go.
Home, so, so far away,

And family hopefully, to see again,
But will never be__ like it once was.
They, much the same; but not me__
Where, has the old me. gone?

Here again, comes, the enemy__
Another mother's son, I take away!

Observation

When, looking at life,
Most tend to look back__
To, yesteryears.
For, they are mostly fact__

Except, if one, polishes them,
To reflect ego's, version of truth__
And, then who will know the "Truth?"
Only the dead! And, they speak not.

Without "truth", life, is like "tares in a field,"
A weed of little__ or no value at all.

Waking of the Mind

The World is in chaos again,
It seems this is the way, every day.
The "good," try to make things better__
The "others" seem to, like it another way.

Let's hope, God has his way__
And, Satan sees not, another day;
Simple words, but truth stated.

The next verses, touch on thoughts__
Of history's__ days and times__
In War and Peace, and "work and play.

Amen, is the word, I say.

A Sailor's Dilemma

I sail today in memories and dreams
As salty tears now shed,
For never again be back__
On rivers, bays and ocean spreads,
For now, those days__
Are gone, and never again to spend.

But, if I could I would,
For, I miss the aroma,
Of the changing tides
That comes on the waves,
And the blowing gales oer the sea,
And the beauty, of the painted sunsets,
Reflected in the sky and waters found__
Always a solace to me.

But, in honesty shared__
Never thought when my time did come__
Ashes for me to be,
For that was not the way,
Of my generations present and past,
Who in burial grounds, hither, and yon__
Resided under tablets, of stone.
With life's dates to see.

But, wonder now,
It a thought for me to best__
Be," ashes" made, and then to share,
A grave with the love of my life__
And a scoop or more,
In a reef to store,

Where creatures of the salty brine,
Could find a home of sorts,
And, share fellowship with me.
Yeah; if I could, but share__
My love for both__
One with family, in woodland solitude__
And the other __ in the tidal reach;
How better I ask, could my Spirit spend__
Those, long moments in eternity?

Moments Not Wasted

In the ebon darkness of eventide,
Tween midnight and dawn,
With no moon to discern,
Storm clouds coalesce and abide,
I awake__ and do rise.
For a chill, races down my spine,
A feeling of dread__ puts me on edge.
For Death, marches,
Throughout Humankind.
Tis not that "it" chases me__
But, in time, perhaps will.
Though, I feel for you;
I think I hear, that demon speak__
And, tis your name, those lips exude.
Show no fear__ but run and hide,
And, perhaps more time alive__
for you will be supplied.
Thank me not, Tis, what one can do for another;
Now that you are a new friend of mine__
This I hear, from the spirits hovering near.

A Boater's Reverie

If, around waters, one abides.
for any length of time__
A breed apart, they become;
For borne, is an internal need__
On, the sea, or any arm thereof, to be.

There is no use to fight it,
For if honest, it is from humanity born,
There is an ebb and flow, in some__
Building until on a boat they must be,
To feel the water's movement,
And, the sense, that they are free.

Thus, held, in a warm embrace,
A different feel, have for GOD above__
And Poseidon, the king of waters below.
This a reverence for both__
refreshed, in every, tidal flow.

One seems. to pray, much more__
When upon a boat deck__ found;
As, the wind and spray,
Like, a baptismal touch and kiss;
To, each boater's cheek and soul__
Delivered, a welcome when found.

So, hear this prayer,
Echoed from the world of water,
To you, oh Lord above,
And, to Poseidon below___
Oh Master, accept our gratitude__
for the air we breathe,

And, each day, thus allowed.
Bless our family, who have helped__
make us what we are__
And, as we travel, near and far;
allow us new friends to make__
To brighten life, on our way.

We thank you for this country__
That has given us freedom known,
And, for the fellowship, of many souls, that helped us grow.
We beseech thee, to make us worth the challenge__
For better men and women to be.
And, make, us, good stewards__
of all waters and lands, granted us to see.

📖

Vista Scene

There was a time back when__
Life and living were racing then,
And, I chanced upon, a mountain high__
And, an opening on that mountainside,
Where few trees, hid not, the land below__
And the valley, in beauty, in sunlight showed.
The sky was of azure blue,
The sun painted all, in colored hues,
The distance down gave prospective,
To each tree, field and animal__
all, took my breath away, but, knew then, as now,
In those moments, my life did change.
Tis worth the effort and time,
For you, to find__ moments near the same___
For tis then to know, GOD speaks to you.

📖

Tinkering With Time
(A lesson for all days.)

The best that can be said,
As an explanation of "**Tim**e:"
As, the calendar pages have turned__
Is to say__ when, the Sun, rises,
It's day! And when below the horizon goes__
Is darkness, thus night, is the time arrayed.
But, actual time__ minutes and such,
Seem to take on more importance__
As a place in life__ each day.

A, truth, just to keep you, from forgetting,
What a privilege it is for you,
And was for your ancestors__
To have been granted space,
On this "Orb, "to breathe the air".

Humankind, over a long period,
Has studied, nature, and realized__
That this planet of ours.
Is not quite symmetrical in shape;
But, with math, science,
And, the brains gifted to humans__
The facts gathered make living here,
More than just a possibility for mere existence.

Making a long-convoluted history, a bit shorter__
Because, of boats on the waters of the world,
And the necessity of plotting true locations,
On maps and charts__
Noting things about the Sun, and "Time,"
Common sense and mathematics__

The Art of: Navigation was developed__
Note, how centuries of study__ flashed by.
Now you could learn much with these facts,
But with a, twenty-dollar watch,
Or, an Atomic Clock, __Keep yourself, on time, in time,
Most of the time you are alive!

And, you can learn much in depth,
For, I remember, the fun it was,
When learning navigation and "time."
So, it is up to you, what you want to do,
But here are some facts as reminders,
Or, perhaps much that is new__ to you!

📖

Tinkering With Time - Chapter 2

**Tick Tock, Tick tock,
So says the grandfather's clock__
But, few of humankind, give, it much though__
In this day and moment,
As, its worldly, game, is continued to play.**

Pick any day in "time",
And spend these moments__
As a reminder, that you, as an "Earthling"
Are lucky, that to be!

And all aspects of "t**ime**" are a gift, to thee.
Take, a clock at Longitude 0° in London at NOON,
And, a clock, is then 8 AM in New York,
And his clock, in LA, will say 5 am, same day,
But her clock near, New Zealand, is midnight 180° E,
And, ready to begin, a new day and date__

Confusing, as it appears__ but correct,
To meet, the needs, on, a westward, rotating, Earth.
And, with correct, times at each 15°
At that given moment__ around the Globe.
The Sun, _ our life-giving SUN, seen.
This scenario, each DAY__ to be replayed__
There are, a lot of pieces in this "puzzle,"
That had to be just right__
Or what we know of the world today,
Would have never come into sight.

Part, of the story is earthly creation,
Beginning, as a new planet in space,
Much to do with: size, shape,
And the good, and goods available for use,
Under a universal Sun,
Plus__ the introduction, of humankind,
And there, somewhat, brilliance__
Of mind, to be found,
Have been allowed, a role to play.
Billions, of what we humans call years,
Have elapsed, in this universe of "ours."
Changes (and up-grades) came at an ant's pace!

The earth kept "time," in rocks and trees,
And, chemistry if you please!
Time, in the first, millions of years, was basically__
Sunrise and Sunset__ for all forms of life;
Then, came cave people, as far, as we know.

In the many millennia, they stumbled and grew,
Most likely traveled, the wilds of a single land; **Pangaea**;
Before this "orb" looked like anything we now know.
When the sun rose in the morning__

Humans, got up, and when the sun went down,
Went to their caves, and slept; a thought, but fact,
Then as each year passed,
Humankind, in knowledge grew,
And, things about life and living
Became clearer to view!
Soon "time" with other things__
In importance, we then knew.

But as the years marched on,
As wonderful as "Earth" was__
Its imperfections became known__
And, challenges for the future, arose.
But the changes that came about,
Were in small steps,
Increments, one after the other.
New knowledge added to old.
Found in ink, on pages in history shown.

There were many days, and decades:
From the Ox cart to the Automobile,
From the sod hut, to the High Rise,
Or most anything you can name.
Let us here, note, and accept, history,
As the doing and the done.

And look to the aspect of "**TIME.**"
And, its importance__ to humankind,
That has, affected, life, as we know it.
And, apparently will, continue until__
Nature, bids__ man, must go!
Maybe, Global Warming & Climate Change,
Are, the beginning of the end?

Tinkering With Time - Chapter 3

From human's, first days,
On the Waters of Earth,
And then going hither and yon__
On the seas of the world,
A means of navigation was imperative.

Latitude, using sun and stars,
Guided boats east and west__
But, "longitude," for, north and south,
A different challenge indeed.
And, "time" it took; an answer to find.

With "time", "in time" knowing, "exact time"
Was a major part of the answer__
Not as simplistic as it sounds__
But with sextant, and "a sea going clock."
A branch of mathematics, a slate, etc.
Location of places, around the word,
Were established.
(A fun thing, for all to heed.)

A place finally accepted as a start:
"**The Rose Line**," in London town,
At the Royal Observatory, in Greenwich,
With an: arbitrarily, established 0°.
Set Longitude's 360: vertical to each pole.,
180° W + 180° E
On Charts, the whole wide world, around__
Yes, a 24-hour Earth Day, divided into 360°,
Gave 24, 15° zones, starting at 0°__
Keyed on a chart if you please,
To 180°, in the Pacific Ocean,

Where a new day and date come into play!
Then, continues & reduces, by 15°, eastward,
(180° -15° = 165° East__ till 0° is reached, again.
This took; many ticks on a clock,
But many humans together got it done!
Then came the late 1800s,
And, in Great Britain, and its dominions,
Steam train travel was big business,
And, had imperative need for, accurate,
Timetable, scheduling, across various time zones.

So, heads they did gather,
And with brains that mattered,
A solution to the challenge was ascertained.
Zones were already established,
Basically, what was needed was adding "Time."
This to serve not only Britain, but also the world.

Thus, the Earth takes 1 hour,
To travel the 15°, in each Time Zone,
And, every 1°, = 4 minutes of time__
So, with a sharp pencil,
Time, anywhere, can be computed.
If you learn the facts, the answer to find__
Even if the Earth Globe, isn't perfect,
Common sense, with, physical understanding,
Is required in clocking time.

And, latitude of a different type is required__
To make time, an accurate measurement!
In London, for example!
0° puts London into two time zones,
Thus, taking, 7.5° East, and 7.5° West,
Where, all of London is in the same Zone.
Other, exceptions in Time Zones,

Throughout the Globe, are also in place!
Now, these words, in lines thus found,
Are in no way a scientific effort profound__
But, a verse, like lyrics of song,
To remind you, of "time," to you that belongs!
And while the premise is somewhat on track,
For full details, **Google on your handheld**,
Will give you, all the facts!
And thus perhaps, get you to fully understand?
The great gift of "<u>**time.**</u>" for you is there.
That is yours; between birth, and final demise,
And, a chance, for you to say "Thanks"
To whatever deity, you subscribe.
Thus ends Our Tinkering with Time!
Some facts not defined but somewhat rhyme?
Oh, and today, Electronics eases locations to find.

Nothing is Forever

There is always, someone, somewhere,
Who, will be "better" than you__
In something, or many things,
No matter how good you do__
This is called life! Be not angry or abashed,
Know, that you, helped, blaze a trail__
For them, a "clue" to find, a direction, to go__
For, one day, in your shoes__ they might be;
And doing your best, is a noble goal.
Then when you have given your all__
Find a challenge new, and do better,
in a new day.

The Essence of Time

There was a boat fire the other night,
Someone's dream is ashes now;
Me, I feel a pain within,
You see I can still remember___
Times on board, and winds a-howl.
Mornings of sunrise, nights at anchor,
Friends rafted together,
Wind; reefed sails__ wet days & nights,
Crashing waves, quiet times,
All different, but good when a float.

There were night sails from Jersey,
The Atlantic, & Delaware Bay___
Hard into the wind,
Lakes Erie and Ontario,
And many other rivers and bays.
I thank God, for my sailing days___
And the times, so granted.
For they. sail through welcomed dreams___
More times. than you would ever guess.
Today, those, memories are, of the best.

I hope and pray, those now___
"Owners of Ashes," if they so wish;
New boating adventures, come their way___
And good memories, they for years collect.

Cry not, *when your crossing, of a deck is "done,"*
But keep the memories alive and well___
Second best; but fodder, for unnumbered dreams___
Replayed. & reminders of unforgettable times.

Each, a Story Tell

The Book of life, when paging through,
See, in my chapter__ there is yet, much to do,
Room there is, for words and verse__
In space, uncluttered, with common curse__
This I had hoped my legacy would be,
To help generations, I never to see!

If but actions I can make,
And ink in, helpful lines,
And tell true the story__
Worth the time, it takes to rhyme.
And, share with all, the right word to find.

Yes, to read; each and every line,
With value for life, there, to find,
And make, an enlightened person,
Whom the world, think a gem is found,
Then, my effort and time__
Invested wisely, and peace be theirs & mine.

But if my effort, a work not well done,
Who would invest, the time, it to read.
And, if not, why should I proceed?
And yet, this a work, I hope to leave,
To pay for the breath, through life I received.
And the learning from others, provided to me,

I wonder if you too, feel this way__
That humankind should and must,
There, debt repay__
For all that was given them__ along life's way?
I have a feeling, that those of you.
Who believe, this premise__ be true,

Will gather together, in place and time___
And review, how better, now we could be.
And the thought to me now does occur,
There must be a way, the good we discuss,
Can be gathered, and given___
To all generations, in the future, following us.

So, nothing is wasted___ as was done,
Throughout Earth's tenure in days now done.
This, a good thought for the future found___
If can be assured, to be done somehow.
What do you say?
About the good in people
We have nurtured along our way.
Would, you agree, that we could better do___
if we on Earth, were allowed to stay?

📖

The Feeling Within

True joy, is in giving;
Not the getting___
For when getting, once gotten,
Sometimes, then is the forgetting.
But when giving,
The smiles and heartfelt thanks,
Become most times, true, gratitude.
And, the joy when selecting;
Is replayed over and over, as memories;
When, recalled in future times___
as part of, both actions, once taken,

And recalled, in future again & again!

📖

Cover Under the Stars

How well, I remember, my love of tents.
Long before, my starting of school.
When down we would go,
To the family shore,
That later I knew was on Dobbin's Creek.
Where my father, with "Amoco Banners,"
Made me, my first "pup Tent."
Then bought a teepee, red & white for me.

Those times, and that place,
Where truly my "salad days"
Never, to be forgotten.
As an only child.
I needed no other playmates.
And, when the shore was sold,
At the out- break of World War two,
A piece of my heart, there remained.
For there, on the grass, among the trees,
Now know, that was one of the happiest__
Of times, for me, that would ever be!

Those sunlit days, and early nights,
Then, recall awaking, in my bed__
In first, morning light__
Now know__ it was my dad's doing!
I don't recall now__
Whatever happened__ to the banners,
And the teepee of red and white,
But both live in my memories.
The shore was gone,
But my time in tent, went on and on!
For in Scouting over many years__
They covered me, on trails,

In camp and, even when in the military.

My wife, sewed, from a plan,
In a "Boys Life reprint, I gave her,
A "one-man" backpacking gem.

If I can find it and note names and totems,
Of those old friends, inked_
After, their Woodbadge training, done.
If so, maybe instead of passing it on__
I'll take it, when I finally go,
and if UP__ maybe then, with, my bride,
She will get a kick to see
How well, her workmanship,
Lasted, over more than a half century.
Likely, in no more tents will sleep.
Nor carry on trails to delight!
Those days and taut line hitches,
And, friends together, on stary nights,
Are captured memories now__
I thank God, for each memory find.

Better to be Good

For most in humankind, better sleep,
Is gotten when good is given__
Than when 'bad' is employed,
and utilized to capture a moment,
just because "one" can, and does__
for some day, the Piper Must be paid.
Think not, then look at history!

Future Review

Oh, to be able to do,
What a decade ago, I could, with ease__
And, now, those projects, once started,
Suffer a pause and now, sit un-attended__
Dust covered, with no action seized.

Is this no longer, a request to be asked,
For too much time has passed__
Cannot, the doing, still be done?
Or, the possibility of success now dismissed
Lost, with the gift of age__ that has come.

Dejection I do feel, but I cannot complain;
My run through life__
Has surpassed many I have known,
But deep within; more I wish to do,
Things and opportunities,
To, bring to a successful conclusion__
Is it too late for me,
Should, this I leave to others now__
Who in their youth, better can see & do?

I do realize, it is not always,
For, what we want or wish, that we get.
And, if in time it is to be nothing__
We should be thankful
for those things, already gotten,
That have, graced our lives, for the better.

So, may I, tonight find a place__
That is safe for my head to rest.
But, if that is not, in the cards__
May my demise__ quickly be.

And, cause few ripples.
In the lives, of those__ known to me.
But, if additional portions of time,
Are, allocated, I will do what I can,
To use it wisely, to my very end.
And, try and find the spirit and drive,
Of the time of decades before__
And leave a record___ second to none.
Hope, that's not asking for too much. more?

Realization

I think, I shan't or can't, any longer do,
What I know must be done.
My brain tells me, yes__
But, my body screams__ *"forget, it, chum."*

My days of doing,
They are almost completely gone__
My one true hope__
For which prayers extend__
Is, for an orderly transition,
From breathing; to none.

My, wish, is this; it to be quickly done.
And my gratitude, be passed__
To every Earthly one__
For the days, they and GOD, let me run.
But, if not yet time__ I want them, understand__
That is more than "fine for this person me.

Chesapeake Icon

Before too many more page's fly__
And, forgetfulness rears its ugly head__
An, Icon should have some ink about it, spread.
For near two centuries on the Chesapeake Bay,
It has serviced, ancestors, and those of today,
And, more ink on white paper might be overdue__
So read you now, and remember__
A bit history, touching a truly an iconic vessel known.

When "R" in the months on the calendar written,
Oysters, are of interest to be getting,
The normal daily Skipjack "uniform," seen__
Boots and many times, rain gear, zipped up tight.
Of course, other adapted to any weather in sight.
Seasonal efforts, of oysters__ eight months long__
The other four, "to ready" boat for next season long.
Skipjack sails, seldom pristine,
Only when "new," in whiteness gleam__
Show the color of a working-boat__
That, "Dirty gray" to her Captain__ a pretty sight.

Now, when blue crabs in mud for winter go,
Crab traps no longer baited and out of sight,
Moved to shore and cleaned,
Painted, stacked and then wait__
For the next spring season, and baited.

But now as September looms,
The Skipjack, readied, its day to bloom.
Are scrubbed and preened__
And for work to begin__ but first;
A rendezvous; to race, and share a bit of time.
Decks, yearn for guest, in dress up clothes,

To share the fun and competition___
But, racing, in these "boats of time!"
Is a serious business__ you'll find
And winning, is a thing of pride__
is, somewhat the badge of honor,
Those, sails, of workboat, gray colored grime__
It's been that way for more, then, a century of time,
And, hear prayers for a wind__ a small gale to find.

Rendezvous, over, winner crowned.
Oysters for eight months, hand dredged,
More now, scraped from bottom, up__
Piled on deck, sorted or dumped,
Then to shore, sold__ and eaten up!

Watching them work, their daily routine,
Plays a symphony of centuries seen__
Tells the history of the Oyster & Skipjack__
For many, wait for a tasty dinner or snack.
Think you about, this iconic boat,
Its, main sail "huge"& boom quite long,
Its shallow draft, in water, to somewhat deep.
And, so stable and strong, requirements meet.

No engine aboard, for in the past, not allowed__
After, the oysters are gotten,
Its, dingy, with motor, will push it forth.
These, are "Queens of the Chesapeake."
But from hundreds, once__ now, just a few around.

Take the opportunity, to give one a try__
Contact, Richardson Museum in Cambridge
And, even take a ride.

Following the Theme

Bees, trees, and butterflies,
And snow-white clouds,
In God's azure sky,
Make for life, always better to see__
Always better__ for you and me!

Tomorrow, we hope, for an even better day,
But if not, we will smile and pray,
And, try much harder in every way,
To live a life, that all would say__
Is the kind of living, good people do.

Life is not easy__ but is good,
Oh, if only all could,
Live the "**Golden Rule**,"
Throughout all, their days,
Think what goodness, would be displayed.

No more wars, for death of the young,
And talent lost, from bullets, and guns.
And all efforts put forth__
Into, making, this, a better, world__
Never before__ truly done.

God's plan__ from days back when__
Stupidity of humans, finally to end,
Before, humankind in chaos__ gone.
And this our orb of "Eden,"
Lost a second and last time.

Think you, not__ this could come?
Take the time to look around,
See God's gifts, here to find.

Wonderful things,
Like Bees, Trees and Butterflies,
Just a few of many, you never, realized__
And," forget not" Clouds in Azure skies!
That give humans peaceful moments to survive.

📖

A Reminder in Time

Our actual "Time" is based on the Globe called Earth.
Adjusted to the rotations westerly made,
And, to the Earthly Orbit around the Sun.
Which mathematics, its answer claims.
It serves us well on this "patch we live__"
Can, humankind, adjusts to another place?

This, Earth, is a true "Eden;" forget it not.
But to lose it, "**without change**," cannot be in doubt;
And, if the loss would become, an actual fate__
Could we find, planets other; to live on__
with one another; equal, to that, of Earth?

So, I ask in all candor, be it not better__
To stop Climate Change & Global Warming;
and, bits of plastics' inundation of the Oceans?
And save this gift of gifts, of Godly, resources__
for yet, unnumbered generations__ yet to come?

By working as one__ could we not stay here; together,
On this "Eden" long ago given; then to try__
Somewhere in space other__ living, with no guarantees?
Doubt not the truth, in these words as written__
For they, it seems; "to you, was a "gift given."

📖

A Thought Given

I need to speak of Earthly things,
For my time, I'm sure
Flees, on speeding wings!
At times, me thinks, too many days,
Have passed__ in unlikely ways__
And, wasted was the time, freely given.
Is the loss of time__ due to aging?
But, "Age" isn't a person,
Tis just a thing, that lives within;
And, stays and stays, until demise__
Then disappears, from seeing eyes.

Age, always adds, never subtracts__
Takes time used, and increases__
To, already totals counted.
And, smiles and counts another digit,
On every anniversary that is visited.
And, hears not the plea__
"Hold the years but not the living."
Understands not, there is no forgiving.
Nature me-thinks, has an evil streak,
It sticks to one plan, never changing__
A seed, a bud, full blooming, & dying,
Never allowing a second trying.
How hard, to, give all__ a second time of breathing?
Knowledge gathered then, in time escorted.
I know, I know, then Nature be concerned__
More than a second coming, might be requested?
When, eternity's plan, is already perfected.
Unless, humankind, again be tested?
Would, God that chance, at another time __ bless it?

Time and Travel

My days are rushing by,
Someday I know__
No more good or even bad will do.
Tis the same for every mortal living.
No one gets out of life alive.
Thank GOD, this a problem, resolved.
But here, is a, conundrum that's pending;
A challenge never ending;
for each mortal, a different, situation--trying.

When once life has ended,
Does all, the good recorded on your, record,
get inspected; before your final __
up or down, is selected?
Now I am not accusing any "Heavenly Body__"
Of devious, doings, when reviewing,
But, can, all get a gander at the judge's record__
Before a sentence is reported?
And would consideration be considered__
Before final direction is commanded?

If you are one, who sees the need__
to let truth be expressed__
There is always a "question",
Of what you should or can__
Put in "ink" on paper__ to be digested.
For truth could anger, a liar, to distraction?
I am one who gives naught, for another's reaction.
Truth to me, should be the words supported.
Then maybe from HELL, one day I to heaven transported?

I wonder if they noted, my fine legacy I delivered?

A Dog's Tale, or Tail

The sun was rising__
This through the curtain, could see,
Heard the lid of the trash can,
Hit the alley with a bang,
And, knew the "dog" was back.

It was his breakfast time,
And, he and I played this game.
And, he was looking up at me.
His tail wagging,
And if dogs could grin,
His was wide as it could be!

First it was just garbage,
He would gather,
And then a breakfast for he,

And, no longer dumped the can,
Just eat what I prepared for him.
And, believe it or not, clean up his mess.
He was smart, one. smart canine.

Knew now, he was a guest each day,
And he and I this game we would play!
I opened the gate, and in a chair sat,
Where he would come after eating,
And lay close to where, I sat.

Well, next he got a bath,
And showed he was house broken,
And walked with me each day,
And that winter, he moved in.
And that__ was more than 10 years ago.

One day, he brought a gift to me,
A, puppy; a splitting image of he!

And another day down the road
I found the two of them at my bed__
The younger woke me up,
And, the older, now my old friend,
was dead!

And the younger and I,
Buried him lovingly in the yard
And, "Deuce" that was his name.
We were together, a decade or more.

And you can believe it or not__
One day, "Deuce",
Brought a puppy to stay,
And the puppy was named "Trey."

And, life went on, I'm glad to say!
Till there came another day.

Now, I hope my son,
Will accept the new puppies,
That, in futures, years seem to arrive!
They are quite special,
But__ it will be my son, to decide.

What a story and legacy to have.
And, you can believe it or not!
But none better I say__
The tale over the years told to me.
By the way__ I'm my father's son!

Family Christmas

Bees, trees, and butterflies,
Tis that time of year,
When counting down the days to Christmas,
And realize, no ideas have yet received,
For gifts to give, to my granddaughters,
Nor for my son, and his bride,

I scratch my head in wonderment,
At the opportunity missing
By those four, to "fleece" this old man__
For some extra dimes!
So, I guess they want me,
To spend what I would have spent,
On myself, and, those wild women__
I like to think of as mine.

But that is a dare, I not to do,
If I want to rest next to "bride"__
When, my life is finally through.
So here is a decision, made__
I will give what I got as kid;
A stocking with some tangerines,
And a pair of socks or two,
And a railroad train, if you would wind it up,
That on tracks, went around and around__
And, and tooted very loud.

And, I was damn happy, with this,
If, no, switches and coal, were given me!
Was it not, I heard you say___
Oh, you think this is a game to play.
so. Just send you, all my bankbooks,
In, registered mail. and the four of you,
Think that would be the right thing to do?

Well maybe. so,
But then all the people, I owe money, too,
Would be chasing, the four of you__
Now that idea, has real merit to me.
But I guess I should thank you__
For in the family, you allow, this old man, to remain.
S0, wish you a Merry Christmas, Ho, Ho, ho!

The Wild West

I, once, upon a horse quite wild__
I, my butt in a saddle found,
At least, for a few seconds__
Before high in the sky was thrown,
And, headed, for the hard, hard ground.

The good news was, I saw no bull,
with long, horns; pawing, the ground__
Just snorting, & waiting, there for me.
When the ground, I accidentally found.

But, even so, I, quickly surmised__
and, realized, the, life of a cowboy,
was not for me. So, I, moved from__
Texas to California, as an actors' agent.
The money and female company was better.

And, a different kind "bull" no horns.
But you can keep the salads,
it's__ Still, beans for me! Yippy cy A.

A Verse-ist's Sharings

But me, writing in verse,
On things to be in play__
And, capturing the information,
That will set the pace, for my next day__
Keeps me "young," and in the game.

Is my thinking frayed?
But, I admit, daydreams come,
Of those times, when I was__
On top of my game.

Memory is sure a pure delight__
And, so was the youth,
Now, for me, lost from sight.

But I welcome each new day,
And hope "good" I can continue to do,
As dues, paid, for the breath I use__
That, to me__ a measure of my worth.
But what, is not retained, does seldom return,
And I worry, what was at stake;
That I, no advantage did take__
Leaving only, an empty ache.

We know so much as humankind,
And yet so little, that comes to mind.

There are things, that at times
Seers and Sages do get,
And, smarter they seem, than you and I,
Tis perhaps, that we refuse__
To open, our minds, for all details, that do get by.
Will all of life__ we one day understand?

Or is that not to be__

Caused by the teasing of an entity__
Who far above, we pathetic souls,
Pulls the "strings" of command.

Tis a large, large universe, beyond__
Earth's stratosphere,
Where a billion years has,
Passed on by.

Who is to say, maybe someday__
We will know __
Who with us__ is truly, allied?

Observation

When, looking at fact___
Most tend to look back;
To, yesteryear.

For that is mostly fact__
Except, if one polishes the truth;
To reflect "Ego's" vision & version,

But Truth is the Truth!
Unless one day, what thought true,
Be found false;
And bruised and tarnished reputations,
Is the fact now applied!

Idea Reception

The time I find, to welcome thoughts,
Is in the morning dark, before the sun,
Gets its start__ to rise,

That is when, this head of mine__
Can grasp ideas__ & welcome words, as a prize!

But honest I must be__
I now, catch not all that should be caught,
For at this time in life, too much new,
Comes too fast__ for this older me.

But I do the best I can,
To make a note__ more than, just now and then,
To nail down, the gist of,
An elusive idea, before it slips away__
And, returns, not ever __ again.

This helps me, as a reminder __
To tame, much, that would escape,
Of items new, touching, my world's scene.

And, yes, the sheer amount of new__
Arriving, in every 24__
Bedazzles__ much of my every day.

But, grateful, I am,
To be a small part of the race__
For most of my generation,
Can no longer keep pace;
Because. of challenges, most old folks face.

Eye, On The "Race(s)"

The good news, is__
Tomorrow, has a chance, to be another day__
If this world, of ours, is, so blessed, to be;
And, we are granted a new sunrise to see.
Don't laugh for we know not__
When breath, no longer for us will come.
And seldom we give that option thought__
We take for granted, "old," is our gift to get.

But, why, should that be?
Who are we___ a god?
How egotistical, an assumption we assume.
And, then abuse__ Nature's gifts.
We allow war to exist,
We assume others are less than we,
And, refuse to allow brotherhood__
Its rightful place, in every life.

The question should be__
Why and how long__
Should humankind, be allowed__
To remain on this: "Eden," in the sky?
How patient, should we expect__
Our, deity will be, with humanity?
Before he, or she; says "done" to start anew.

Perhaps, that Deity, will think__
Tis easier to start from naught,
To give, a new breed of humans a try!
Then have to fix so many broken parts.
Don't you think it's time, to toe God's line?
Will that you truly do?

📖

Carried Pieces

Like all, one day__
I had a reason to houseclean,
So, to speak __my wallet of some age,
And, what I, found,
Was bits and pieces, all part of my life!
I was carrying around,
For no reason, I can't explain.

Take for example, Incased in plastic,
In calling card sized,
Easily readable, phone list,
Of, members of an organization,
To which I still belong.

On this neatly done 2 X 3 card,
Forty-four Members names listed,
Dated is some 9 years ago__
Not that long ago, but long enough,
For 8 to have "gone to God,"
And, most no longer having boats,
But half, still as members, subscribed.

Well, the point being made:
Members come and go,
Interest flourishes and wanes,
While, many friendships do remain.
But why are the others,
No longer active, still on the roster, allowed?

"Time" stands still for no one or thing__
Group rosters are historical reminders
Of who, we were, are and could be.
But carry, a list, not-up-to-date__

Can you answer me—why not?
This was just one item,
In that wallet of mine,
More than, I like to admit,
I am carrying around each day.
And it wasn't and isn't,
The oldest item there!
But proves if you're like me,
And, I think many are.
The past, good or bad,
Is comfortable, & our safe retreat__
And, no additional work is invoked.

Yes, a little, of one's life tucked away,
That someday, will be__
Fodder for the recycle bin
As each, in life will be__
Just a name on a list,
Of, little, value, but perhaps, missed.

Just words to make you think,
How much history resides with you__
And though written down,
Clutters your space and time now around,
A gift for others, someday maybe__
But like said, little use today.
And perhaps that too, is a bit untrue!

How many memories would a name bring__
As the years," zip" on by.
If a moment or two, were invested,
In person, place and time__
Me, many times, seek the face of a friend.
And a call, makes life right again.

Stormy Night

It was, in the middle of an ebon night,
When clouds, scudded across the sky,
And winds rattled the window, panes,
And heavy rain began its downward fly!

When, the Hand Maiden, rose to her job,
As Satan danced on her breast,
And, pained her very soul!
For dark hallways, awaited, her steps.
The youngest of the young,
She was of the household.
Each room must be touched,
To close the windows, tightly,

And draw each drape and shade,
To, keep the ghosts_ far away.
And, the rainwater out,
And mildew at bay!

Fearful she, but must duty attend,
Or the mistress, find torture to spend_
In this castle of old,
Cold and more than terror find_
For the Hand Maiden
Just another castle "slave!"
Oh why, had she been abandoned_
Orphaned, and cast away?

There are many kinds of slavery,
And it is not new to humankind_
And unfortunately, exists even today,
And, takes free movement away.
With chains of different kinds.

Hundreds of years,
After the "Hand Maiden" __
Had withered away!
Tis, only luck of the draw,
That being a slave is not your calling,

So, what are you going to do;
To assure, all slavers are denied__?
Life and living__
For, if it is not you, who will,
Why should they__
Those purveyors of angst;
Worry their minds, about__ any other?

But you must__ know it; or not__
You are, your, brothers' and sisters' keeper,
As are all of the world's people,

And, a day will come, an answer be required.
Just thoughts to stir your thinking,
And perhaps open your eyes,
To the path you should be taking!

Of course, you need not__
Do anything, and just walk away.
But know, someday, the Devil will call.
And then, you will become a slave__
After all.
A story, a tale, history in fact,
There, before, then, and since__

It is past the time, for all slavery to end.
If not, you __ who then__ this to do?

Life Facts

Think you, that your time on Earth＿
Is a free ride?
Then, how mistaken you are＿
True, you did not ask to come.
Others made that decision＿
Without consulting you.

Of course, you may not,
Have even been in their plans,
But here you are,
So, maybe not the first choice,
But a choice you now can make＿
Stay＿ or do away with Earthy Time!

Ah! A choice is presented＿
And, humankind, their price, established,
Pay, or go away. "Ain't," life great and grand?
Rules, made by unknowns, throughout, time;
during the days granted to you.

WAIT: Maybe you are the one＿
To, make life better＿ for all?
But, a "Free Ride," Don't be dumb.
What, is true, If, allowed, life is what you make it.
Being here is the chance you get＿

And actually,
Being here, is a great opportunity,
And, arriving＿ is a gift in itself.
Ask Satan＿ he'll tell you＿
Or is Satan, only God in disguise?
What a world; but it is, your "prize."

Counting Time

As I mark the decades,
That I envision are mine__
Looking into the future,
Many, so many, I find,
These could be mine, or maybe not.

Yes, I know this is supposition__
For no "Seer" am I, making a claim,
And, all life can be lesser;
Then what Fortune Tellers'__
Chrystal Balls or palm-readings, lay claim.

We, at the mercy, of Nature's omnipotent__
plan, and, if smart, will obey its dictates.
Or death maybe our, final stand.

Who is to guide me__
Through these wild waters of life?
Is GOD truly my Lifeguard?
Or am I, Poseidon's next guest__
Having only the Devil at my side?

I wonder and wish, If to GOD
I can speak__
And, if an answer in words receive?
Or am I, like all others; needing, to seek,
And look to Nature for answers to find?
Should I, be prepared; just to "Count Time?"

Or, Is there, another, choice to be mine?

Hello?

A Woman in My Life

She, always special to me,
For I, the only grandchild to come;
Never much was told or knew__
Of her family tree, till just years ago,
from an old family Bible. The first landed,
in Burlington, NJ, 1677; met by_ Wm Penn.
By 1700, 53 families total, 31 in Lancaster PA,
and 21 crossed to MD.

She of flaxen hair, till, teen years fled,
Family of double, digit numbers,
Varied ages, well spread.

School days done before a century new,
And married three years before,
Her twentieth birthday drew.
A mother of four, three to live,
By the first decade done!
And the calendar showed 1910.

I remember her long hair,
Always, in a daytime "bun."
Her dress was always Quaker like,
Her shoes, laced ankle high!
And, wise she was.
Throughout, our near 3 decades of history.

She passed to heaven's gate, In her eightieth year,
When I was in the New Jersey hills,
Schooling, for a new career__
And me, not yet thirty.
And, much of her history still didn't know,
Until another after, few decades did go.

It was, just the way, of family then__
For quiet" was just family done.
And, I now, wonder why I didn't ask?
So much lost with each rising sun.
But when my "bride" passed half, century on__
Time, I took at photos looked,
And what written, history could be found.

Too bad I asked not, those years ago,
So much more today, would, like, to know.
And, I no better than they,
For this history, I am not writing down!

She left me a note in an envelope sealed:
"So much more I would, like to leave you,
But love is what you get, she said!"
She didn't realize, how much,
She gave to me, in our shared years__
But so much more__ in my life with her,
I would, have liked to have had.

To: Evva Gertrude "Kinsey" Ogle__
A Grandmother like of which,
All should have had. 1883-1963

Thought Messenger

So much I would like to know today,
That was lost in the rush of yesterday.
And, most tomorrows, I feel__
Belong to others, and are not mine to reveal.

Sustenance

I see no place, to stop and eat__
The briers and brambles, Leave little room,
For me to spread a blanket down,
On a grassy knoll,
Where comfort could be found!

Am I always, to be upright, to dine__
Am I not to "sup" with linen fine?
Is mine to be__ always, to use:
Broken and cracked crockery,
And dull knives, and three-tined forks,
And noggin carved by me for wine__
Is this my fate, until I dine no more?

Why is not a place set for me;
With people, in concert,
With whom I should be?
Have I not lived a life, worthy to find;
My education, somewhat impeccable,
I have been told "at" times.
Is there bias, because of my, color,
Or, my religion, or race__
What kind of world is this place?

Where even, the talented and untalented
A fair opportunity cannot find__
To live, their lives as they devise?
If there is a GOD__
Then life, should be equal__
For all humankind.
Science has shown, all humankind__
came, from the same "Tree of Life..."
With blood match; insides; all interchangeable,

Outsides differing, because of:
Geography's need, for adaptation__
Where each human was, initially, placed.
Is there a "GOD?"
Then, why is in not__
That equality, for all, known, and shown?

What will it take___
To have, GOD's world
See, all in brotherhood__
Occupying__ the, Earth's Space;
Is, this not, a promise, for r all to have__
And, if not__ why not; May, I ask?

Winter, on the Bay

This past winter was hard__
Icy cold winds, & frozen ground,

Snowfall for days,
Most humans are in, not walking around!
The docks at the marina, most empty__
Boats; in cradles or on jack stands found.

Work-boats out, unless frozen in__
To, wait, for, ice breaking __ sounds.
Just another year for the watermen,

For this is the life chosen__
So, they, take it, as it comes,
With hot coffee, and if lucky a sweet bun.

To Understand

There comes a time,
When one must stand.
If not to do, he or she__
Will not pay their dues,
And, forever then rue that day__
When things or a thing, left undone,
And forever know__
A debt, to repay, begun.

And, forever more, to know__
"Interest" be owed to fellow beings.
For we all belong,
To the "Tree of Humankind."
And, brothers, sisters are we,
And, it is not just a village__
But in its way, the whole world,
Who raises each of us __ (you, I & me).

If, we, view not,
That, life is a valuable gift,
Granted to each, throughout, one's days,
And, we see not, a debt, be owed,
To all fellow beings__
Lost we become, in place and time__
And we, be a liability,
Rather than, a force for good.

Sometime it must be seen
That each must give back,
In kind, and on demand,
For things received.
Like, breath, shared__
To belong to the brotherhood of man;

If not, ask why__
Why, were you, ever here?
Not all will to this respond,
But the special ones,
Find, courage in line to stand,
And, understand,
All are, their brothers and sisters__
Under their skin!

"For fellow man" heroes, not all can be,
For if they were, the world,
this world__ too good to see . . .
And none in perfection,
Can truly live;

While, thinking; the "best, Is: "**ME.**"

📖

Selection

If we but look with care,
At diverse family, gathered around,
I, truly wonder__ how many,
We would admit to the outside world__
Were kin, we would claim?
We might wish it were all,
But, that could, or would be __
A lie profound.
The saying is old__ but wise:
You can pick your friends,
But, family, come with no vote applied.

📖

Shakespeare Maybe
(A bit of fun at the Bard's expense; or is it?)

To be, or not, to be!
Perhaps, that is truly the question?
And not the ambiguity, posed, by __
A writer/poet, long gone.
Be it truly, William Shakespeare or not?
The question of the authorship at the time
Still rages today, and lacks:
A response, satisfactory to "all."
Raising hackles and sores, that fester.

But whom-so-ever put that ink to fool- cap__
All would agree__ is damn fine writer.
But, was with, bits, of worm droppings__
Centuries, before, you birthed into existence;
So, why, even consider, a controversy, so old?

Maybe because, a truth, is involved__
For the first one under discussion,
Most likely a philosophers' question;
And the other a politicians' probing__
Concerning his/her unfilled pockets.
In reality, it seems to be about credit__
To be allocated by one's favorite or another.
And who has more votes than the other.
But there is slim evidence available,
From a time so far back,
Perhaps never fully documented at the time,
Too bad; Computers, weren't in vogue.

Wouldn't the "Bard" have enjoyed this repartee?
So, you do believe Mr. "S" was the writer so praised?
Just a moment of levity,

While we wait for the Pandemic,
To, dispense with the non-inoculated__
So, the COVET won't keep reproducing.
I wonder, if the Bard would,
Swap the Black Plague for the Pandemic?
(note the time written) Me thinks, he too smart,
To swap into this chaos of today__
But you, might like to imagine it "be" so?

Just the musing, of a semi-drunk, Poet of sorts!
But you have to admit,
One or two thoughts are pretty good.

Who Says

Tomorrow is another day!
So, say the pundits!
Who will, steal as much, "eye, and ear time"
From you__ as they can!
But they speak the truth__
Or so they say.
Like, as long as our planet,
In orbit stays circling the sun,
Another birthday you will have,

Some time in its run.
As long as breath you find,
To make 365 days.
And Earth doesn't decide to spin away.
Maybe tomorrow will be another day!

Winter Walking

President's Day, on the calendar find,
High School Senior year, soon behind.
Our Scout Troop's winter mountain trek_
A favorite weekend, always of mine.

This year: cold, so cold the weather_
Wet, was sleet pelting down,
Gray, the low hanging clouds,
On the road after school,
Parents dropped us off, head of trail,
Slippery, the trail, so steep,
Night, was well upon us,
No moon in the darkening sky_
This, our annual winter walk,
Our hike into this season well found.
Love of the outdoors,
A strange, compelling, love indeed.

How far, the cabin before full dark;
Steps quicken, a time yet to go,
Thoughts now, of dry, warm clothes_
Hot stew on wood burning stove,
And, a cup or two, of hot chocolate,
And, fellowship, at the fireplace, truly nice.
The cabin CCC, built, in Depression years_
Long before we were born. Thick walls, solid;
Ours to use, on many, woodland nights.
Time on a trail_ so, steep_
Seemed, to pass, on fractured wings.
But, soon, distance, made good,
The cabin somewhere in the shadows stood.
A faster pace_ put us at the door.
Unlocked and all inside,

Wet gear stacked fireplace's side.
Firewood, piled last summer,
Opened, the draft__ and lit her off.

As I looked around, realized, for many____
This, our last winter trip, in this moment in time!
Our Scoutmaster nodded, as he read my mind.
High school over in just months,
Scouting days, nearly done.
Then it will be the younger kids,
In our place, who will reside.
Funny how those memories,
Of the last eight years.
Come unbidden, to the fore!
Sweet pain of that moment,
Played before my eyes__
This time of growing,
Soon to be done.

These wonderful days of Scouting,
Will be left behind__
But not those friends,
Of field, mountain and stream,
Who, I will see, hopefully forever__
Or, at least in my mind.

But, these faces of now,
Thirty years hence,
Maybe most not recognizable__
As life, plays its game.
Our Scoutmaster was standing beside me,
And, said: "Tis hell growing up, or old."

"On my honor, I will do my best - - -

"If you were lucky enough, to be a Scout__
With great memories stored,
Hopefully, they are yours__ forever more."

The SM said: "But if you are like most of us,
Life and age will play its tricks,
And, oh, how you will prize any notes__
The few, you wrote, and put safely away,
For they are the "gold of your treasure__ saved."

If, It Could Be

If I, were granted three wishes:
Me thinks__ the first would be__
To be able to remember, all the things,
Told, learned, and taught to me__
In those days after birth took place!

I think, the second would be__
I would be smart,
And a "Wise Man" of my time.
And, do great things,
For my family, country and the world.
And, maybe, help all__ have a better life to find.

But unfortunately, no wishes have I,
And only a slight knowledge, retained.
But give me credit, for wanting to help all,
A better world build, to claim.

Discipline, Makes It So

If one, wishes, to__
Make one's monies' count,
The formula to consider, is this:
With all (every penny) received,
Put 10% immediately away,

Plus, every 10% until your retirement day.
Invest it; never, to be touched—
Until you, put *work away*,
For this money it isn't yours;
But, for the_ one, you, will be__
On that future day.

It will be amazing, the amount__
That, compounding, interest and wisdom,
Becomes, during, the rest of your working life__
That will come into play, and then-- pay you.
Let you not; think, to do this is a drudge__
For once you start, It becomes a part of you.
And to miss, even once, Is like, a breath__
Forgotten, to breath in.

After this, 10%, you put away,
The 90% is yours, to live on, and even invest more__
"Until Retirement comes your way."

Yes, 10% now and until your retirement day,
Untouchable, and a responsible way,
To live life, assure, ensure & insure,
those future days, when no longer income,
But the interest earned, comes your way.

Smile Remembered

These few words, if that is to be,
Are shed with tears,
And, dredged from memories,
Recalled of the time once then,
And, some from days,
Much newer, but we much older seen.

This to a friend, a brother-in-law,
A kindred spirit of long yesterdays___
He, now passed, too soon,
With much living yet to do,
But now, called to service,
As all of us, one day will be.

He was one, we were sure,
Not yet to go!
Challenges he faced, but attitude high___
But his number "came up."
And, called he was,
For, a job, GOD, now tasked him for.

And, I hope and pray,
He gets a job in "Sales,"
And he finds, his old ball glove___
And decks of cards, to shuffle and play,

And his golf buddies I bet,
A chance for another round or two,
And maybe, a hole in one___ long overdue,

I have known Butch,
Since my early teen years,
When at a Sunday school, picnic___

A "First Aid," bandage applied,
On a cut as I recall__
Most likely, well earned, or deserved.
And, now seven decades,
Have passed over the dam!
For that (Red Hair, to No hair),

Very little, changed over the years__
And all will miss him__
But, time now__ to say fare-thee- well.

Me, I will miss the voice over the phone,
The more than abundance of emails,
The together times, and, so much recalled __
During, the great run we both enjoyed.

He was always the little brother,
At whose antics, his sister__ my wife;
Smiled and shook her head, at the doings,
Of that one, with head of red.
Maybe, more stories, someday his sons;
and others will gather to share laughter,
and tears with the next generation.

So, too Miss Lucy, Matt, Mark,
Tom, Jimmy, Bob and their families__
We in our own way, shared that adventure,
To be remembered, on life's way.
So, whenever you, smell cigar smoke,
Or order a cold beer, and a dozen crabs,
Toast the life of: **Nelson "Butch" W.**,
my Brother-in-Law; and know,
He'll be smiling back your way.

History If Not Accepted

Spun was the web, that deceit wove,
No time, was for peace, just war__
How, wild dogs, like those sociopaths,
Who, caught the eye and ear,
Of, unscrupulous people,
Would, tender moments, to, hear the words,
That the tyrant, spread__
And, many could not understand.

The world in chaos, once again, is fed.
Why so few would at the time, stand up,
To hold the "shield of right,"
To deflect, the spears__
Of lies, and arrows, of discontent__
Fired by the then numbers__
That would put down, the meek,
Thus, stay, their evil purpose__

For, by not reacting as should,
As, psychotic leaders on the platform, stood__
Put untold numbers, at death's door.
History records time and time again__
As, so much talent, was put to the sword__
And, again and again, this story is written.
And then, the Psychotic leader __
Bullies his herd, using a faithful few,
And lights the fire of discontent__
And, with uniforms and banners strutting,
In decade or decades following,
Plays havoc with lives of millions.
And, smiles in evil satisfaction.
Then, many times, ends up__ taking his/her own life.
So, no retribution__ is forth coming.

The oblivious, that history's records,
Has long been written and given.
Takes too long, for "good" to support
That death and war, years do collect
When if only all would grasp__
The acceptance of *"brotherhood,"*
Is the cure, "GOD, long ago__ did project.

If nothing is done,
Poor "Earth." may face; Armageddon.
And somewhere else,
Stupidity, like weeds will again be sown.
Every "YOU" is the answer to a better world.
But this, you already know.

📖

Words, Somewhat Like

All it takes, for Evil to exist,
Is, for the good to sit on their asses__

And spur the animal, in the wrong direction.
And, before they can, get going to the right__
To where good *can* be done
A lot of the, bad stuff, has well begun__

And, when "crap piles up," It takes a lot more effort
To get rid of, the smell & blight.
Tis a shame, when just a bit of righteous goodness__
Would, have been __ all that, was, needed__

to make the world right.

📖

That Book

What do you think,
When the Bible you see?
And, you pick it up,
And hold it in your hand.

Is, there an awaking__
When you turn a page__
And, the words in verse, come alive?

Do you accept each word as Gospel truth__
Or, does much therein, cause you concern?
When some passages,
Cause a slow burn__
Because "science"
a different idea applies?

Can you forget what angst you feel,
When, history comes to say.
A politician, (like Constantine),
And others, who think themselves "Holy,"
Played Scrabble and inked down words__
Putting more, than their two-cents into the fray?
Or do you accept the Bible,
Understanding its worth, in truth and verse?
And, see it as the salvation of man?

Tis, the most published book ever,
In languages of most every land,
But still not accepted, by all__
Can this__ you understand?

Or, is it like others of its ilk__
Just, another type, of fairy tale?

Or is it a tome for all times,
That talks of a world, to be found.
In languages, many will read and heed.
Or is it a book of truth; many thinks is a spoof?
Until, in their last breath, is seen as truth.

It was first written by hand,
Then, the printing press, became a fan__
And, many learned through it, to read,
And still, many, its content won't, believe,

But I have been told__
When "WAR" is at hand,
In, fox holes few atheists, can be, found!
And, prayers are the words heard__
Too bad, it takes war, the smarts to understand.

What a world, is ours to have__
And while sin, too many crave,
Were we not, endowed, with__
The, common sense, to see__
The wisdom "the book" does contain?
For, centuries, its word, has spread__
Even though not all, every word believed.

At least, should not all__ the **Golden Rule** live?
"Do unto others, as you would have them, do unto you__"
That even a fool, its wisdom can conclude.
Yes, other religions with words scribed,
Try their brand of good, and most aren't bad,
But, better if, **"the book"** was in every hand?
And, maybe yes, or maybe no,
Time will see this as the plan__ to command.

Those Days

Those days of boots and paddles,
Are lost to me now___
But, not the memories, of times,
When adventure, beauty and friends,
Kept, my mind, in wonder,
And, my body, on path, river and trail.

But now I ink pages,
Of short stories in verse,
Of times on wilderness trail,
In, mountains, above tree lines,
And, the feel of paddle in hand,
And, tiller, with water at the rail.
In support Not-For-Profit groups,
And me, remembering, days of my youth.

Yes, my days__ are now fewer,
But still a good day's work I put in,
And, while no woodland trails wander__
Closer to home, I catch many a good view.
I, converse with friends__
And with service, hope, pays for breath I use.

True I miss those days gone now.
And, the many, years, with the BSA,
And, older friends who mentored me,
But, have no regrets to say__
For my run through life,
Was, more than fine__
And, my door is always open,
For those that want to stop by__
And, ask about this and that.
That they should give a try.

But, have to, admit, yearning,
of those times never dies.

When the Time Comes
(An older friend, shared these words with me.)

I fear not dying, my concern, Is the length of:
"Time and Pain;" that Death demands__
when making. a call.

What need is there to delay,
For. the one, slated to go;
Or, for his or her family and friends,
Who, share those sad moments__
Between breath and demise.

My, answer: is NONE. We enter this world,
In pain a mother is subscribed__
And then, most, with some pain__ abide.
But why__ when life is to be denied__
Is more pain__ applied?

In, Death, me thinks the Sadist;
Should be the one, denied;
And as a gift__ peace be granted__
To the dying, earned throughout, one's lifetime.

(I think, that friend; was both right, and wise.)
Peace be with you and yours.

Moments for Growth

In these now, my dotage years_
Thoughts come with wisdom clear.
And I, if a wish come true could have,
Would wish, that each __
He and/or she, would, in a canoe,
With paddle in hand,
Two weeks would spend,
With unknowns, and friends__

For, I have seen and remember__
Many young adults, over dozens of years,
Growth received, in that time span;
With, many miles, on wetted lands__
Pull their weight, and gain "God's" truth.

What knowledge, would absorb,
On, sunrise of morn and moonlit night__
What growth in stature earn.
What wonders, in dealing with others get__
What judgment in all things,
Would be born.

The list of things, captured for life,
Is, greatly touched upon;
How one would change, for the better__
Does boggle the growing mind.
The canoe, and the water found,
A classroom of life, where credits abound.
The people of the crew,
Mature, and become friends for life.

The days, how many, you count,
See 100s of emotions come out.
And long after the paddle is stored__
Memories resonate,

And return, as "Mile-Posts;"
Forever more.

I sense, you do not believe this is so,
And, all I can do is wish for you,
Is the challenge one day, you would know.

Yes, youth, is the best of times__
But anytime, is the time to go.
Tis not an easy experience to have,
And maybe not ever for you__
But remember this is my wish__
And, I wish only the best for you.

Old is this one,
Who, has had to put__
The paddle down,
But, shares with you__
What he/she knows is true.
Is worth, more than gold in hand__
May you the "mother lode" do find.
And, carry, life's memories with you
For, the investment, that suggested,
Will pay dividends each day,
When facing, life's trials;
As you do learn__
to carry through.
"Amen" I say,

For this prayer I share,
For each and all, throughout your tomorrows.

Spyglass on Life

When looking, toward "tomorrow__"
One tends, to forecast,
In somewhat factual-fiction;
Of a future desired, not yet arrived__
Nor, assured in coming, to pass.

This opens one up, to be judged,
On, the veracity, of, dreams, plans.
Insights, facts and the like.
Could this be__ one's bucket list,
Of things, you want,
And perhaps, need to do__
To make life, a perfect delight?

All tomorrows, are a gamble__
But living in tomorrow, Is the life to be.
If not__ little is left for you__
But, sadness and demise,
And, both will one day, catch up to you.

Living, in yesterdays, unfortunately, reflects;
An, unwillingness to face the thing called "CHANGE."
That restlessly, awaits you. to recognize__
that all, tomorrows are the place for you.

This is your challenge__ No matter your age,
A conundrum, for sure__ but, worth the effort;
For you to, undo its secrets!
Life and living, never stand still.

Keep this in mind, for each new challenge__ found.

The Gift of Gifts

A thought about life of Humankind,
and the years that followed the swamp;
and cave life, and Eden, and all the rest, to date__
We, never asked to be here on Earth__
and all that came with the last billion years__
I doubt most humans ever thought of that?
Or if they did, felt; someone, somewhere likes me__
Or NOT. Perhaps, tis worth giving some thought

What are the odds, that a mass of gases,
And bits, of this and that, of space trash,
Arrive in a spot, and remain, and not__
Continue, on, a trip through, a Universe gigantic.
As, a fiery, "bit," to the end of it__
And, in time, did whirl and spin, and make;
A semi solid ball, almost perfectly round.

Each period, rotated a full turn on an axis.
And at the same time, gravitated into a ___
Circular orbit around a colossal gas sphere.
And, the Orb, in its turn, had light and then dark,
And it's changing angle throughout the orbit,
Provided, four different seasons each year.

The time was right, and solid ground__ found,
With waters, salt and not. & breathable air.
Humankind was tried, and by using brains__
and knowledge gained, on this Imperfect Orb,
Received time a life to find.
However, I wonder if that Entity, would consider it again__
After seeing the mess, humankind, has made, this time?
Hope is a proof we must show is ours.

The Man I Am

*(On a wall of, a building old, these words,
Painted, more than caught my eye.)*

I am, I am, the man around,
The man you see in every town,
The man that climbs, the mountain high,
Whose, head is in the clouds up in the sky.

Yes, I am, I am, walking tall__
Always up, for one and all,
I am, I am a man for all to see;
Shoulders square__ marching proud;
For. my country, In which, I believe!
And I, claim; it's good__ even now,
As, chaos challenges one and many.

But at times, looking hard__
One, must strive, that good; to see.
But if we truly search, good will;
Raise their hand and volunteer.
And things, better, will be seen.
Like in yesteryear, in this country known.

This is a special place, that cannot allow__
After, more than, 200 years, it die in disgrace.
When all that is needed, is Yankee ingenuity.
and Common Sense, to do right.
That, in someday soon, can and will say__
There is good, in, humankind__ seen like yesterday.
That writer the kind of leader, we need today.

www.ingramcontent.com/pod-product-compliance
Lightning Source LLC
Chambersburg PA
CBHW060204050426
42446CB00013B/2987